Derby
Entertaining

Traditional
Kentucky
Recipes

13-digit International Standard Book Number   978-1-934898-01-7
Library of Congress Card Catalog Number   2008923656

Cover design and book layout by Asher Graphics
Photography by James Asher except where noted below.

Photograph on page 4 by Janet Worne, *Lexington Herald Leader*
Photograph on page 6 by Frank Anderson, *Lexington Herald Leader*
Photograph on page 92 by Tim Broekema

A special thanks to Adrian Wallace and Ashford Stud Farm; Kentucky Horse Park; Dale Rogers, Marnie Walters and Woodford Reserve; and Ron Garrison, *Lexington Herald Leader*. Thanks also to Larry and Denise Casares, David Dominé, and Susan Wiley.

Manufactured in the United States of America

All book order correspondence should be addressed to:

McClanahan Publishing House, Inc.
P.O. Box 100
Kuttawa, KY 42055

270-388-9388
800-544-6959
270-388-6186 FAX

www.kybooks.com

Bluegrass tradition is deeply embedded in the hearts of Kentuckians throughout the world. Nurtured by the riches of the land, filtered and purified through natural limestone, sustained by strong cultural heritages, painstakingly developed into our champion thoroughbred bloodlines, blended into our smooth Kentucky bourbon, it is celebrated during the many events surrounding the famous first Saturday in May, and finally culminating in the aptly labeled "most exciting two minutes in sports."

We celebrate the Kentucky Derby at the race track and in our homes. The Run for the Roses brings the horse culture and the culinary arts together to the full attention of entertainers throughout the region. When planning a 4-course dinner or a cocktail party, *Derby Entertaining* has the perfect menu for you. This collection fits any and all celebrations for this big event. From **Silky Sunshine** and **BLT Dip** to **Bourbon Pork Chops** and ending with **Mint Julep Cheesecake,** all of these dishes are sure to make your taste buds tingle.

Kentuckians celebrate and cherish the Derby traditions that have become a rich part of Bluegrass heritage. When spring is in full swing and race day approaches, use these great culinary delights in your own *Derby Entertaining*.

Photo by Janet Worne

MENUS

Call to Post Hors d'ourves	7
Grandstand Dinner	13
Backstretch Brunch	20
Triple Crown Evening	25
Starting Gate Servings	35
Champion Breakfast	43
Around the Turn Favorites	49
Fast Track Features	57
Basically Bluegrass	63
Front Runner Classics	71
Daily Double Delectables	77
In the Money of Course	85
Odds on the Meal	93
Off Track Temptations	103
Place Bet or Show Samples	109
High Stakes Sensations	117
Photo Finish Buffet	129
Index	136

6

Call to Post
Hors d'ourves

Traditional Mint Julep...9

Starting Gate Smoked Salmon...10

Benedictine...10

Bourbon Bread...11

Chocolate Kentucky Bourbon Balls...12

Traditional *Mint Julep*

1 cup sugar
1 cup water
1 cup mint leaves
Crushed ice
Kentucky bourbon
Mint sprigs

Combine the sugar and water in a saucepan and bring to a boil. Cover and cook without stirring for 5 minutes. Remove from the heat and allow to cool. Place the mint leaves in a bowl and bruise the mint with the back of a wooden spoon. Place the mint in a jar and add the sugar syrup. Cover and chill for 12 to 25 hours. Strain the mixture and discard the mint when ready to use. Fill frosted silver mint julep cups or old-fashioned glasses with crushed ice to serve. Add 1 tablespoon of the syrup and 1 ounce of the bourbon for each serving. Stir, garnish with a mint sprig and serve with a half-sized straw.

Makes 20 servings.

Smoked Salmon

**8-ounce container chive and
  onion cream cheese spread**
**One loaf of dark pumpernickel
  party bread, sliced**
Sliced, smoked salmon
Horseradish

Spread the cream cheese on individual slices of party bread. Place a small slice of salmon on the cream cheese. Squeeze a dollop of horseradish on top of the salmon. Serve immediately.

Benedictine

1 medium cucumber, peeled and seeded
8-ounce package cream cheese, softened
1 small onion, finely ground
1/2 teaspoon salt
Dash of hot pepper sauce
Mayonnaise
2 drops green food coloring

Finely grind the cucumber pulp and press out the juice until the pulp is fairly dry. Mash the cream cheese in a mixing bowl using a fork. Work the cucumber pulp into the cheese. Add the onion, salt and hot pepper sauce. Add enough mayonnaise to make a smooth, easy-to-spread filling. Add enough food coloring to make the cheese a pale green and mix thoroughly. Use for finger sandwiches or as stuffing for celery.

Bourbon Bread

3/4 cup raisins
1/3 cup Kentucky bourbon
1 1/4 cups butter, softened
1 1/2 cups sugar, divided
6 eggs, separated
2 1/4 cups self-rising flour
1 1/4 teaspoons vanilla extract
1 cup coarsely chopped pecans

Soak the raisins in the bourbon for 2 hours. Drain and reserve the bourbon. Add enough bourbon to make 1/3 cup. Cream the butter and 1/2 cup of the sugar until light and fluffy. Add the egg yolks, one at a time, beating well. Add the flour in thirds, alternately, with the bourbon; mix until well blended. Stir in the raisins, vanilla extract and pecans. Beat the egg whites until soft peaks form. Add the remaining sugar gradually; beat until stiff. Fold the egg whites gently into the bread batter. Line the bottoms of 2 loaf pans with waxed paper. Spoon the batter into the pans. Bake at 350 degrees for 1 hour.

Makes 2 loaves.

Bourbon Fermenting

11

Chocolate
Kentucky Bourbon Balls

1/2 cup softened butter
16-ounce package powdered sugar
1/4 cup Kentucky bourbon
1 cup chopped pecans
Four 1-ounce squares semisweet chocolate
Four 1-ounce squares unsweetened chocolate
Pecan halves

Cream the butter and gradually add the sugar, beating well at a medium speed. Add the bourbon; beat until smooth. Stir in the pecans. Chill and shape into 1-inch balls. Cover and chill for 8 hours. Combine the chocolate in the top of a double boiler. Bring to a boil, reduce the heat and cook, stirring often, until the chocolate melts. Pierce each ball using a toothpick and dip in the chocolate. Place on waxed paper to harden. Gently press a pecan half on top of each ball. Chill until the chocolate hardens.

Makes about 48 bourbon balls.

Grandstand Dinner

Around the Turn

    Beer Cheese Soup...14

Fast Break

    Black Bean and Rice Salad...15

Hall of Fame Pork Chops...16

Kentucky Sheet Cake...18

Around the Turn

Beer Cheese Soup

2 cloves garlic, minced
2 tablespoons butter
4 cups chicken stock
1/2 cup all-purpose flour
1 can beer
1 pound grated sharp Cheddar cheese
1 teaspoon seasoned salt
1/2 teaspoon freshly ground black pepper
1/8 teaspoon cayenne pepper

Sauté the garlic in the butter in a heavy saucepan. Add the chicken stock and bring to a boil over a medium heat. Stir in the flour that has been whisked in the beer. Cook until slightly thickened, stirring constantly. Add the grated cheese, salt, pepper and cayenne pepper; stir constantly until the cheese has melted.

Serves 6.

Black Bean and Rice Salad

Fast Break

2 cups cooked black beans or two 15-ounce cans, rinsed and drained
2 cups cooked basmati or jasmine rice
1 cup olive oil
1/4 cup lemon juice
2 cloves garlic, minced
2 green onions, sliced
Salt to taste
Pepper to taste
2 tablespoons fresh cilantro
Romaine lettuce

Combine the beans and rice in a large mixing bowl. Mix the oil, lemon juice, minced garlic, green onions, salt and pepper in a bowl. Stir in the cilantro. Pour the dressing over the beans and rice, mix lightly, cover and chill. Tear the desired amount of Romaine lettuce into bite-size pieces. Add the lettuce to the bean, rice and dressing mixture and mix gently when ready to serve.

Serves 8.

Pork Chops

4 lean, thick pork chops
1/2 cup flour
2 teaspoons salt
1 1/2 teaspoons dry mustard
1/2 teaspoon garlic powder
2 tablespoons vegetable oil
10 3/4-ounce can chicken and rice soup
10 3/4-ounce can cream of chicken soup

Dredge the pork chops in a mixture of the flour, salt, dry mustard and garlic powder. Brown the pork chops in the oil in a large skillet. Place the pork chops in a slow cooker and pour the soups over the top. Cover and cook on low for 6 to 8 hours or on high for 3 to 4 hours. The soups make a wonderful gravy for mashed potatoes or rice.

Kentucky Sheet Cake

1/2 cup butter
3 1/2 tablespoons cocoa
1 cup water
2 cups all-purpose flour
2 cups sugar
2 tablespoons baking soda
2 eggs
1/2 cup sour cream

Combine the butter, cocoa and water in a saucepan. Cook over a low heat until the mixture comes to boil, stirring often; remove from the heat. Combine the flour, sugar and baking soda. Add the chocolate mixture and beat until smooth. Add the eggs and sour cream; mix well. Pour the batter into a coated 10x15-inch baking pan. Bake at 350 degrees until the cake tests done. Ice with Kentucky Frosting.

Kentucky Frosting

1 cup butter
4 tablespoons cocoa
6 tablespoons milk
16-ounce package powdered sugar

Combine the butter, cocoa and milk in a saucepan; cook over a low heat until the mixture comes to a boil. Remove from the heat, add the sugar and beat well until the sugar is dissolved and the mixture is fluffy. Spread over the Kentucky Sheet Cake.

Backstretch Brunch

Country Ham Balls...20

Sun Shines

   Bright Strawberry Bread...20

In the Lead Sausage and Grits...22

Derby Day Cheese Soufflé...23

After the Race Apple Squares...24

Country Ham Ba

4 cups cooked, ground country ham
1 cup dried bread crumbs
2 eggs
1/2 cup milk
1/2 cup vinegar
1/2 cup water
1 cup brown sugar
2 teaspoons prepared mustard

Combine the ham, bread crumbs, eggs and milk in a bowl. Form into small meatballs and place in a shallow baking dish. Mix the vinegar, water, brown sugar and mustard in a separate bowl. Pour the mixture over the meatballs. Bake at 350 degrees for 25 minutes or until brown.

Sun Shines
Bright

Strawberry Bread

3 cups all-purpose flour
1 teaspoon baking powder
1 teaspoon salt
1 tablespoon cinnamon
2 cups sugar
1 1/4 cups chopped pecans
4 eggs, beaten
1 1/4 cups vegetable oil
2 cups frozen sliced strawberries
  and juice, thawed

Sift the   flour, baking powder, salt, cinnamon and sugar into a large bowl. Combine the pecans, eggs, oil and strawberries in a separate bowl; mix well. Make a well in the center of the dry mixture. Pour the pecan mixture into the well and stir to moisten. Pour the batter into two coated 9x5-inch loaf pans. Bake at 350 degrees for 1 hour. Allow to cool 5 minutes before serving.

21

Sausage and Grits

1 cup quick grits
4 cups chicken broth
1/2 cup cornmeal
1 pound bulk sausage, fried and drained
3 eggs, beaten
Salt to taste
Pepper to taste
Cayenne pepper to taste
Canola oil

Cook the grits in a saucepan with the chicken broth; boil and stir until thick. Add the cornmeal, sausage, eggs, salt, pepper and cayenne pepper. Spoon the mixture into a loaf pan and chill overnight. Unmold, cut into 1/2-inch slices and sauté in oil until crusty and browned. Serve with maple syrup.

Serves 8 to 10.

Derby Day Cheese Soufflé

3 tablespoons butter
3 tablespoons flour
1 cup scalded milk
1/2 cup grated sharp Cheddar cheese
1 teaspoon salt
4 eggs, divided
1 additional egg white

Melt the butter in the top of a double boiler. Blend in the flour. Stir the milk in gradually, blending until smooth and thick. Add the cheese and salt. Beat the egg yolks until light and lemon-colored and pour the cream mixture into the eggs. Beat the egg whites until stiff but still moist. Fold half of the egg whites into the cream sauce fairly well. Fold the second half in just lightly. Pour the mixture into a coated soufflé dish or straight-sided baking dish. Bake, uncovered, at 375 degrees for 35 minutes or until the soufflé has puffed up and browned. Serve at once to prevent it from falling.

Serves 4.

23

Apple Squares

1 cup all-purpose flour
1 teaspoon baking powder
1/4 teaspoon salt
1/4 teaspoon cinnamon
1/4 cup margarine, melted
1/2 cup packed brown sugar
1/2 cup sugar
1 egg
1 teaspoon vanilla extract
1/2 cup chopped apples
1/2 cup chopped walnuts
1 tablespoon sugar
1 tablespoon cinnamon

Sift the flour, baking powder, salt and the 1/4 teaspoon cinnamon into a large bowl. Add the melted margarine, brown sugar, 1/2 cup sugar, egg and vanilla extract; blend well. Add the apples and walnuts and stir well. Spread the mixture in a coated 8-inch square pan. Combine the 1 tablespoon sugar and 1 tablespoon cinnamon and sprinkle over the top of the mixture. Bake at 350 degree for 30 minutes or until done. Cool and cut into squares.

Triple Crown Evening

Silky Sunshine...29

Jockey Spicy Snack Mix...29

Hot Brown Soup...30

Down to the Wire Pasta Salad...31

Down the Stretch Bourbon Salmon...32

Lucky Day Green Beans...32

Bourbon Brownies...34

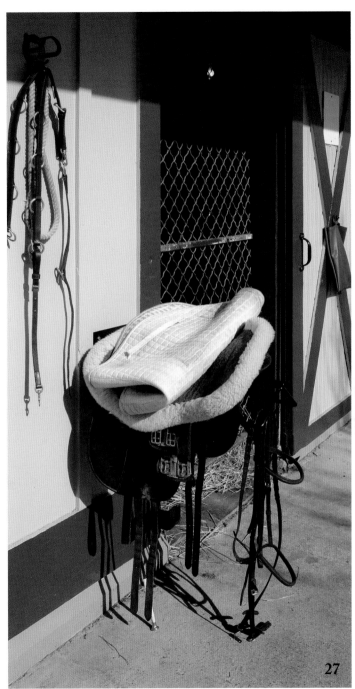

Silky Sunshine

1 1/2 ounces Woodford Reserve bourbon
2 ounces orange juice
2 ounces piña colada mix
1 teaspoon simple syrup (equal parts
   sugar and water thoroughly dissolved)
Crushed ice
Orange slices, optional

Pour the liquids into a cocktail shaker and shake well. Pour over ice and garnish with an orange slice.

Jockey Spicy Snack Mix

4 cups Crispix cereal
3 cups corn chips
2 cups pretzel sticks
2 cups cheese-flavored snack crackers
2 tablespoons taco seasoning
1/2 cup vegetable oil
1/2 cup butter, melted

Combine the cereal, corn chips, pretzel sticks, and snack crackers in a large bowl. Mix the taco seasoning, oil and butter; blend well. Pour over the cereal mixture and toss to coat. Spread the mixture on two uncoated 10x15-inch baking pans. Bake at 200 degrees for 2 hours, stirring every 30 minutes. Remove from the oven and cool. Store in airtight containers.

Hot Brown Soup

8 strips smoked bacon
1 cup finely chopped onion
1/2 cup finely chopped celery
4 cloves garlic, minced
2 medium red potatoes,
   peeled and cut in 1/4-inch pieces
3 cups diced turkey breast
2 cups dry white wine
2 cups chicken stock
5 cups milk
2 teaspoons kosher salt
1 teaspoon ground white pepper
1/4 teaspoon ground nutmeg
2 cups heavy cream
1/2 cup all-purpose flour
2 cups shredded white Cheddar cheese
Crumbled bacon, chopped tomato and
   chopped fresh parsley, for garnish

Cook the bacon in a Dutch oven over a medium heat until slightly crispy. Add the onion, celery and garlic and sauté until tender. Add the potatoes and turkey and cook, stirring occasionally, until the turkey is seared on all sides. Add the wine, turn up the heat and stir to deglaze the bottom of the pan. Cook for 5 minutes and add the stock, milk, salt, pepper and nutmeg. Simmer over a low heat for 15 minutes or until the potatoes are tender, stirring often to avoid sticking on the bottom. Whisk the cream and flour in a small bowl and stir into the simmering soup. Turn off the heat, add the cheese and stir after the mixture has thickened. Adjust the seasonings if necessary and serve with slices of toast and desired toppings.

Serves 8 to 10.

Down to the Wire

Pasta Salad

16-ounce box shell pasta
2 1/2 cups mayonnaise
3 tablespoons Old Bay seasoning
1/3 cup lemon juice
Salt and pepper to taste
1 small sweet onion, diced
5 celery stalks, diced
1 green pepper, diced
1 red pepper, diced
**10-ounce package shredded
   Cheddar cheese**
1 1/2 cups diced ham

Cook the pasta according to the package directions; rinse and drain. Blend the mayonnaise, Old Bay seasoning, lemon juice, salt and pepper until smooth. Combine the pasta, diced vegetables, cheese and ham in a large bowl. Pour the mayonnaise mixture over the pasta mixture and stir thoroughly. Chill overnight for the best flavor.

Serves 10.

31

Down the Stretch Bourbon Salmon

1/4 cup firmly packed brown sugar
1/4 cup Kentucky bourbon
1/4 cup Dijon mustard
1/2 teaspoon cayenne pepper
1/4 cup lemon juice
4 salmon filets
Salt to taste

Combine the brown sugar, bourbon, mustard, cayenne pepper and lemon juice in a small mixing bowl and whisk. Pour the mixture into a shallow dish and place the fish in the dish and marinate for about 30 minutes. Remove the fish and discard the marinade. Sprinkle the fish with the salt and place on a hot grill. Reduce the heat to medium high and cook for about 10 minutes or until fish flakes easily.

Serves 4.

Lucky Day Green Beans

16-ounce can green beans,
   drained and rinsed or
   frozen green beans
1 tablespoon minced garlic
2 tablespoons real bacon bits
1/2 cup chopped onion
Salt and pepper to taste

Place the green beans in a saucepan and cover with water. Add the garlic, bacon bits and onion. Cover and cook over a medium heat for 30 to 45 minutes. Season with the salt and pepper.

These are best when made a day ahead to let the flavors blend.

Bourbon Brownies

1 cup all-purpose flour
1/4 teaspoon baking soda
1/4 teaspoon salt
2/3 cup sugar
1/3 cup shortening
2 tablespoons water
1 teaspoon vanilla extract
6-ounce package semisweet
  chocolate chips
2 eggs
1 1/2 cups chopped walnuts
4 tablespoons Kentucky bourbon

Sift the flour, baking soda and salt in a mixing bowl; set aside. Combine the sugar, shortening and water in a saucepan; stir constantly bringing just to a boil. Remove from the heat. Add the vanilla extract and chocolate chips; stir until smooth. Beat in the eggs, one at a time. Add the flour mixture and walnuts, mixing well. Spoon into a coated 9-inch baking pan. Bake at 325 degrees for 30 minutes. Remove from the oven and sprinkle with the bourbon. Cool and cut in squares.

Makes about 24 brownies.

Starting Gate Servings

Race Day Sippers...37

Breakfast Fruit Salad...38

Fast Break French Toast Bake...39

Infield Cherry Freeze...40

Race Day Sippers

6 ounces white grape juice
4 ounces apple juice
6 ice cubes

Blend all of the ingredients in a blender until very frothy. Serve immediately in wine glasses, garnished with thin slices of red apple skin.

Makes about 4 servings.

Breakfast Fruit Salad

1 cup sour cream
2 tablespoons honey
2 tablespoons orange juice
4 bananas, sliced
2 oranges, pared and sectioned
2 cups strawberries, cut in half
1 1/2 cups granola

Combine the sour cream, honey and orange juice in a small bowl. Arrange the fruit in a glass serving bowl. Top with the sour cream mixture and granola.

Serves 8.

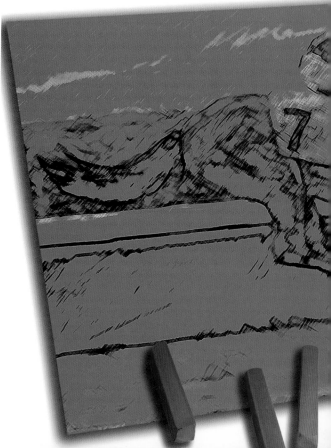

French Toast Bake

12 eggs
1/2 cup maple syrup
2 cups milk
12 slices bread
Two 8-ounce packages cream cheese

Beat the eggs in a large bowl. Add the syrup and milk; mix well. Break the bread into bite-size pieces and spread in a lightly buttered 9x13-inch baking dish. Cut the cream cheese into small pieces and spread out over the bread. Pour the egg and milk mixture over the bread and cream cheese. Cover and refrigerate overnight.
Uncover and bake at 375 degrees for 45 minutes when ready to serve.

Serves 8 to 10.

Infield Cherry Freeze

21-ounce can cherry pie filling
3/4 cup crushed pineapple, drained
14-ounce can sweetened condensed milk
1/4 teaspoon vanilla extract
1/4 cup lemon juice
2 cups whipped topping

Combine the pie filling, pineapple, sweetened condensed milk, vanilla extract and lemon juice in a large bowl and mix well. Fold in the whipped topping. Pour the mixture into a coated dessert mold, cover and freeze for 24 hours. Remove from the mold, slice and serve.

Serves 8 to 10.

41

MENU

Champion Breakfast

Spring Morning Mimosas...44

Out of the Gate Ham Biscuits...45

Winning Ticket
   Breakfast Casserole...46

Thoroughbred Peach Cobbler...48

Spring Morning Mimosas

4 cups club soda, chilled
12-ounce can frozen orange juice concentrate
2 bottles champagne, chilled
Orange slices

Blend 1 cup of the club soda and orange juice concentrate in a blender. Pour the mixture into a punch bowl; stir in the remaining club soda. Slowly add the champagne. Float the orange slices, if desired.

Serves 20.

Out of the Gate
Ham Biscuits

1 cup all-purpose flour
2 teaspoons baking powder
1/8 teaspoon salt
1/4 teaspoon dry mustard
3 tablespoons solid shortening
1 cup cooked, ground country ham
1/2 cup or less milk

Combine the flour, baking powder, salt and mustard in a bowl. Cut in the shortening using a pastry blender until the mixture resembles coarse cornmeal. Add the ham and enough milk to make a soft dough. Turn out onto a lightly floured board; knead for 30 seconds. Roll out to 3/4 inch thickness. Cut using a small biscuit cutter. Place the biscuits on a lightly coated baking sheet. Bake at 450 degrees for 10 minutes. Serve with butter.

Makes 24 biscuits.

Winning Ticket
Breakfast Casserole

1 pound mild pork sausage, cooked
  and drained
1/2 cup chopped onion
4 cups frozen, shredded hash brown
  potatoes
6 eggs, lightly beaten
2 cups shredded mild Cheddar cheese
1 1/2 cups small curd cottage cheese
1 1/4 cups shredded Swiss cheese
Salt and pepper to taste

Cook the sausage and onion in a large skillet
until browned; drain. Place the hash brown
potatoes in the bottom of a coated 9x13-inch
baking dish. Layer the sausage over the hash
browns. Combine the eggs, Cheddar cheese,
cottage cheese and Swiss cheese in a large
bowl. Pour the mixture over the potatoes and
sausage. Bake, uncovered, at 350 degrees for
35 to 40 minutes or until the eggs are set and
bubbly. Let stand for 10 minutes before serving.

Serves 8 to 10.

46

Thoroughbred

Peach Cobbler

11 cups peeled, sliced peaches,
   about 5 1/2 pounds fresh or 4 1/2 pounds frozen
3 tablespoons lemon juice
1/2 cup sugar
3 tablespoons all-purpose flour
3 tablespoons butter, cut into pieces
2 cups all-purpose flour
1/3 cup sugar
1 tablespoon plus 1 teaspoon baking powder
1/2 teaspoon salt
1/2 cup butter
1/2 cup cream
2 large eggs
2 teaspoons grated lemon peel

Combine the peaches, lemon juice and 1/2 cup sugar; mix in the 3 tablespoons of the flour.
Pour the peaches into a 9x13-inch baking dish and dot with the 3 tablespoons butter. Place in
a preheated 400-degree oven for 5 minutes while preparing the batter. Sift the 2 cups flour,
1/3 cup sugar, baking powder and salt in a bowl. Cut in 1/2 cup butter until the mixture resembles
coarse cornmeal. Stir in the cream, eggs and lemon peel. Drop 14 mounds of batter over the
heated peaches and spread each mound slightly. Bake for 25 minutes or until the dough is
golden brown.

Makes 14 servings.

Around the Turn
Favorites

Bluegrass Mushroom Soup...50

Quarter Mile Cole Slaw...51

Beef Parmesan...53

Mint Julep Cheesecake...55

49

Bluegrass
Mushroom Soup

1 tablespoon olive oil
1 clove garlic, minced
1 shallot, finely diced
1/2 cup chopped button mushrooms
1/2 cup chopped oyster mushrooms
1/2 cup chopped Portobello mushrooms
1/2 cup Kentucky bourbon
3 cups cream
1/2 pound brie cheese,
   cut into small cubes

Heat the olive oil in a skillet and add the garlic
and shallots; sauté until translucent. Add the
mushrooms and cook for 3 minutes. Deglaze the
pan with the bourbon; cook until the bourbon
has almost evaporated. Add the cream and
reduce the heat. Cook until the liquid is reduced
by half. Add the brie cheese and heat through.

Quarter Mile
Cole Slaw

1/2 head green cabbage
1/2 head red cabbage
1 Gala apple, peeled and shredded
1/2 teaspoon seasoned salt
1/2 teaspoon pepper
1 carrot, shredded
1/2 cup chopped green pepper
1/2 cup mayonnaise

Shred the cabbage. Combine the cabbage and apple in a large bowl. Season with the salt and pepper. Add the carrot and green pepper. Stir in the mayonnaise and mix well. Cover and refrigerate until ready to use.

Serves 4.

Beef Parmesan

1 1/2 pounds beef cube steak
1 cup Italian-seasoned bread crumbs
1/2 cup grated Parmesan cheese
2 tablespoons olive oil
2 teaspoons minced garlic
1 onion, sliced into thin rings
1 green bell pepper, sliced in strips
16-ounce jar spaghetti sauce
1/2 cup shredded mozzarella cheese
12 ounces angel hair pasta
1/4 cup butter

Coat the meat with the bread crumbs and Parmesan cheese. Heat the olive oil in a large skillet and sauté 1 teaspoon of the garlic for 3 minutes. Brown the meat quickly on both sides. Place the meat in a baking dish, slightly overlapping the edges. Place the onion rings and peppers on top of the meat. Pour the spaghetti sauce over the top. Bake at 350 degrees for 30 to 45 minutes. Remove from the oven. Sprinkle the mozzarella cheese over the top and and heat until bubbly. Boil the pasta al dente and drain. Toss in the butter and the remaining garlic. Serve the meat and sauce atop a mound of the pasta!

Prepare the meat ahead of time and refrigerate overnight. The acid in the tomato sauce will tenderize the meat even more. If you do this, save the mozzarella cheese until the last minute.

Mint Julep Cheesecake

2 cups crushed chocolate graham crackers
4 tablespoons butter, melted
Two 8-ounce packages cream cheese
1/2 cup sugar
1 1/2 cups sour cream
2 eggs
2 teaspoons Kentucky bourbon
2 tablespoons butter, melted
3 ounces cream cheese
4 tablespoons butter
2 cups powdered sugar
3 teaspoons mint flavoring
2 drops green food coloring
1 cup semisweet chocolate morsels
3/4 cup heavy cream
Fresh mint, for garnish

Combine the crushed graham crackers with the 4 tablespoons melted butter in a bowl. Pat the mixture in the bottom and sides of a 9-inch spring-form pan. Bake at 350 degrees for 10 minutes. Remove and let cool. Combine the two 8-ounce packages cream cheese and sugar in a food processor and mix until smooth. Add the sour cream, eggs, and bourbon; mix well. Add the 2 tablespoons butter and mix again. Pour the mixture into the cooled crust. Bake at 350 degrees for 1 hour. Cool and refrigerate. Combine the 3 ounces cream cheese, 4 tablespoons butter and powdered sugar in a food processor and mix well. Add the mint flavoring and food coloring and mix. Spread this layer onto the baked and cooled cheesecake. Refrigerate. Melt the chocolate morsels in the top of a double boiler and add the cream, stirring until the chocolate melted. Refrigerate, stirring every few minutes, until the mixture is thickened like cream cheese. Spread over the green layer and refrigerate until set.

Serves 10.

MENU
Fast Track Features

Cream of Asparagus Soup...58

Bleu Cheese Cole Slaw...59

Winner's Circle

 Shrimp and Artichoke Pasta...60

Peppermint Dessert...61

Cream of Asparagus Soup

3 pounds asparagus
6 cups chicken broth
3 cups heavy cream
1/2 teaspoon salt
1/4 teaspoon pepper
2 1/2 tablespoons cornstarch
2 1/2 tablespoons water

Wash and trim the asparagus; cut into 1-inch pieces. Cook the asparagus, in enough salted water to cover, until very soft and liquid is reduced by half. Strain and reserve the cooking water. Whirl the asparagus and 2 cups of cooking liquid in a blender. May have to do in batches. Place the mixture in a large pan with the broth. Add the cream, salt and pepper; bring to a slow boil. If a thicker soup is desired, mix cornstarch and water; whisk into the soup.

Makes 6 servings.

Bleu Cheese Cole Slaw

1 tablespoon sugar
1/2 teaspoon salt
3 tablespoons lemon juice
2 heaping tablespoons bleu cheese crumbles
1 heaping tablespoon mayonnaise
4 cups chopped cabbage

Combine the sugar, salt, lemon juice, bleu cheese and mayonnaise; mash the bleu cheese to distribute evenly. Toss the mixture with the cabbage and chill for 1 hour before serving.

Sculpted by Jamie Burnes

Winner's Circle
Shrimp and Artichoke Pasta

2 tablespoons olive oil
1 pound large shrimp, peeled and deveined
2 teaspoons minced garlic
1/2 teaspoon pepper
1 1/2 cups chicken broth
1 cup chopped mushrooms
Two 12-ounce jars artichoke hearts,
    rinsed, drained and chopped
1 1/2 cups coarsely chopped plum tomatoes
1/2 cup chopped parsley
2 tablespoons butter
1/2 teaspoon salt
1/2 teaspoon dried oregano
1/2 teaspoon basil
1 pound linguine, cooked and drained

Heat the oil in a large skillet; add the shrimp and 1 teaspoon of the garlic. Cook over a medium heat for 3 to 5 minutes, stirring often, until the shrimp are opaque but translucent in the center. Remove the shrimp, using a slotted spoon, to a bowl. Add the remaining garlic, pepper and chicken broth to the skillet. Bring to a boil; cook for 3 to 5 minutes to reduce liquid slightly. Stir in the mushrooms, artichoke hearts and tomatoes; cook for 3 to 5 minutes. Add the shrimp and cook about 2 minutes until the mixture is hot and the shrimp are no longer translucent in the center. Remove from the heat. Stir in the parsley, butter, salt, oregano and basil. Pour over the hot pasta and toss to mix.

Makes 8 servings.

Peppermint Dessert

2 sticks margarine
4 cups crushed chocolate graham crackers
2/3 cup sugar
12-ounce can evaporated milk
1 teaspoon vanilla extract
1/2 gallon peppermint ice cream
16-ounce carton whipped topping
4-ounce bar dark chocolate

Melt 1 stick of the margarine and mix with the graham cracker crumbs; pat into the bottom of a 9x13-inch pan. Bring the chocolate, the remaining stick of margarine, sugar and milk to a boil, slowly, in a saucepan. Cook for 4 minutes, stirring constantly. Add the vanilla extract and mix well; let cool. Spread the ice cream over the graham cracker crumbs. Pour the chocolate sauce over the ice cream and top with the whipped topping. Garnish with the shaved chocolate, if desired. Freeze.

Serves 12.

Basically Bluegrass

Bloody Mary Pitcher...65

Kentucky Krispies...66

Horse Racing Hot Brown...67

Marinated Asparagus...68

Bourbon Cake...69

Bloody Mary Pitcher

1 cup vodka
4 cups tomato juice
4 teaspoons Worcestershire sauce
2 dashes of hot pepper sauce
1 teaspoon celery salt
1 teaspoon salt
Pinch of garlic salt
Celery sticks, for garnish

Combine all of the ingredients, except the celery
sticks, in a blender. Pour into a pitcher filled
with cracked ice. Serve in tall glasses with
celery sticks.

Makes 6 servings.

Kentucky Krispies

1 cup grated sharp Cheddar cheese
1/2 cup butter, softened
1 cup all-purpose flour
1/2 teaspoon salt
1 teaspoon red pepper
1 cup crisp rice cereal

Combine the cheese and butter in a large bowl and mix well. Stir in the flour, salt and red pepper. Add the cereal and mix thoroughly. Drop by teaspoonfuls, 1 inch apart, onto an uncoated cookie sheet. Flatten slightly using a fork. Bake at 350 degrees for 12 minutes. The dough may be refrigerated up to 10 days before baking.

Makes 6 dozen.

Horse Racing

Hot Brown

4 tablespoons butter
1/2 cup all-purpose flour
4 cups milk
1/2 cup grated Cheddar cheese
1 1/2 cups grated Parmesan cheese, divided
1/2 teaspoon salt
1 teaspoon Worcestershire sauce
2 pounds cooked, sliced turkey
16 slices toast, trimmed
8 tomato slices
16 slices bacon, cooked

Melt the butter; add the flour and stir well. Add the milk, Cheddar cheese, 1/2 cup of the Parmesan cheese, salt and Worcestershire sauce. Cook, stirring constantly, until thick. Place the turkey evenly on the toast. Cover with the cheese sauce. Top with tomato and bacon slices. Sprinkle with the remaining Parmesan cheese. Bake at 425 degrees until bubbly.

Makes 8 servings.

Marinated Asparagus

3 pounds asparagus
Two 14-ounce cans hearts of palm,
   drained and cut into 1/2 inch pieces
1 cup canola oil
1/2 cup cider vinegar
3 cloves garlic, crushed
1 1/2 teaspoons salt
1 teaspoon pepper
Lettuce leaves
Cherry tomatoes

Cook the asparagus in boiling water until tender-crisp. Drain and cool in ice water; drain well. Combine the asparagus and hearts of palm in a resealable container. Whisk the oil, vinegar, garlic, salt and pepper in a mixing bowl. Pour the dressing over the vegetables. Cover and chill for 8 hours, turning the container occasionally. Place the asparagus and hearts of palm on the lettuce leave. Garnish with the cherry tomatoes.

Serves 12.

Bourbon Cake

18 1/4-ounce package yellow cake mix
3-ounce package instant vanilla pudding
4 eggs
1/2 cup vegetable oil
1/2 cup water
1/2 cup Kentucky bourbon
1 cup chopped pecans
1/2 cup Kentucky bourbon
1/2 cup butter
1/2 cup sugar

Combine the cake mix, pudding, eggs, oil, water, and the 1/2 cup bourbon in a bowl and mix for one minute. Add the pecans and mix well. Pour the mixture into a coated tube pan and bake at 325 degrees for 50 to 55 minutes. Pour the remaining bourbon, butter and sugar into a heavy saucepan and boil until the sugar is dissolved. Pour over the cake while still warm.

Serves 12 to 16.

Front Runner Classics

Shrimp Milano...72

Mushrooms Florentine...73

Post Race Hot Brownie...75

Shrimp Milano

1 pound peeled shrimp, cooked and drained
2 cups sliced mushrooms
1 cup green pepper strips
1 clove garlic, minced
1/4 cup margarine
3/4 pound cubed processed cheese
3/4 cup whipping cream
1/2 teaspoon dillweed
1/3 cup grated Parmesan cheese
8 ounces cooked fettucini, drained

Sauté the shrimp, vegetables and garlic in the margarine in a large skillet. Reduce the heat. Add the cheese, cream and dill and stir until the cheese is melted. Stir in the Parmesan cheese; add the fettucini. Toss lightly.

Makes 6 servings.

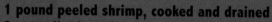

Mushrooms Florentine

1 pound fresh mushrooms
1 tablespoon vegetable oil
1 teaspoon salt
1/4 cup chopped onion
1/4 cup melted butter or margarine
Two 10-ounce packages frozen, chopped spinach,
   lightly cooked and drained
1 cup grated Cheddar cheese
Garlic salt to taste

Remove the stems from the mushroom caps. Sauté the stems and caps
in the oil until brown. Combine the salt, chopped onion and melted butter with the cooked spinach. Spread the spinach mixture in a shallow
10-inch baking dish. Sprinkle with 1/2 cup of the grated cheese.
Arrange the mushroom stems and caps over the spinach and cheese;
season with the garlic salt. Cover all with the remaining cheese. May be
refrigerated until ready to bake. Bake at 350 degrees for 20 minutes, if
just prepared, or 35 minutes if made ahead and refrigerated.

Serves 6 to 8.

Post Race
Hot Brownie

1 cup self-rising flour
3/4 cup sugar
2 tablespoons cocoa
1/2 cup milk
2 tablespoons butter, melted
1 teaspoon vanilla extract
3/4 cup brown sugar
1/4 cup cocoa
1 3/4 cups hot water

Combine the flour, sugar and the
2 tablespoons cocoa in a large
bowl. Add the milk, butter and
vanilla extract; mix until smooth.
Pour the mixture into a coated
2-quart baking dish. Combine the
brown sugar, 1/4 cup cocoa and
hot water; mix. Pour the mixture
over the batter and bake at
350 degrees for about 45 minutes.
Serve with ice cream.

75

Sculpted by Isidore Jules Bonheur

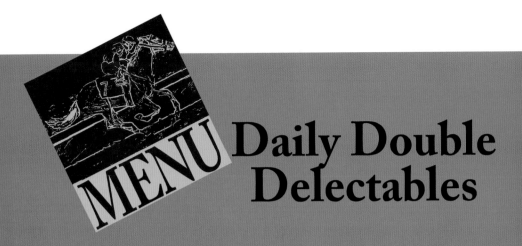

Daily Double Delectables

Derby Day Biscuits...78

Break Away

Breakfast Sandwich...78

Skillet Coffee Cake...80

Derby Day Biscuits

2 cups self-rising flour
2/3 cup shortening
2/3 cup half-and-half

Combine the flour and shortening in a large mixing bowl. Hand mix using a pastry blender until the mixture resembles little peas. Add the half-and-half and stir lightly. Turn the mixture onto a floured surface and shape into a ball. Roll out to 1/2 inch thickness; cut using a biscuit cutter and place each on an uncoated baking pan. Bake at 450 degrees for 10 to 12 minutes.

Makes about 12 biscuits.

Break Away

Breakfast Sandwich

6 bagels, cut in half
12 cheese slices
Apple, thinly sliced
Cinnamon

Arrange the bagels on a baking sheet. Top with the cheese and apple slices; sprinkle with the cinnamon. Broil in the oven until the cheese is melted.

Makes 12 servings.

79

Skillet Coffee Cake

3/4 cup butter, melted
1 1/2 cups sugar
2 eggs
1 1/2 cups flour
1 teaspoon almond extract
Pinch of salt
1 cup sliced almonds
1/8 cup sugar

Combine the melted butter and 1 1/2 cups sugar and mix well. Add the eggs, one at a time, and blend well. Add the flour, almond extract and salt; mix well. Line an iron skillet with heavy-duty aluminum foil. Pour the batter into the foil-lined skillet. Sprinkle the almonds and 1/8 cup sugar on top of the batter. Bake at 350 degrees for 30 to 40 minutes. Lift out of the skillet using the foil and let cool on a wire rack. Do not peel the foil off until cool.

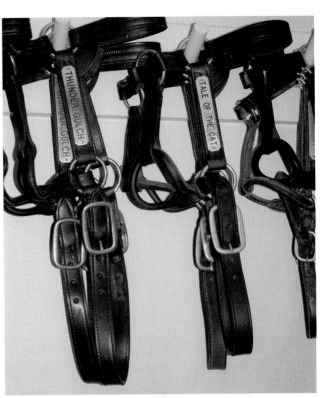

MENU

In the Money of Course

Spicy Brie...87

Baked Potato Soup...88

Traditional

   Kentucky Country Ham...89

Chocolate Chip Cake...90

Spicy Brie

8-ounce wedge brie cheese
15.75-ounce bottle Fischer & Wieser's
 Original Roasted Raspberry
 Chipotle Sauce
Fresh raspberries and mint for garnish
Butter crackers

Remove the covering over the cheese using a sharp knife. Place the cheese on a serving dish and warm in the microwave for 10 to 20 seconds or until the center begins to soften. Pour 1/2 cup of the sauce over the top, allowing it to drizzle down the sides. Garnish with the fresh raspberries and mint. Serve with the butter crackers.

For variation, try a 3-ounce package of cream cheese. Serve at room temperature and pour 1/3 cup sauce over the top. Serve with apple wedges and crackers.

87

Baked Potato Soup

4 to 5 baking potatoes
1 to 2 large onions, chopped
Vegetable oil
1-pound package maple-flavored bacon
One or two 32-ounce boxes chicken broth
Salt and pepper to taste
1 or 2 red bell peppers, diced

Bake the potatoes the night before making the soup and place them in the refrigerator to firm up the flesh. Sauté the chopped onions in a 6-quart Dutch oven in the oil until golden brown; set aside. Cut the bacon into 1-inch pieces and sauté in a skillet until almost done. Drain the bacon and add to the sautéed onion. Dice the baked potatoes and add to the mixture; add the salt, pepper and enough chicken broth to cover the mixture. Bring the mixture to a low simmer and simmer for about 30 minutes. Add the peppers for color. This soup may be refrigerated until ready to eat and reheated. Add more salt and freshly ground pepper to taste.

Traditional Kentucky Country Ham

Many country hams are covered with mold when purchased. Scrub or cut off the mold and rinse the ham with a mixture of equal parts of white vinegar and water. These hams always taste salty. To remove some of the saltiness and add moisture back into the ham, place it in a large kettle, cover with fresh water and soak overnight. Drain and cover again with fresh water. Bring the water to a boil and cook 20 minutes per pound of meat. For best results insert a meat thermometer and cook to 165 degrees. Remove the skin, spread with 1 cup of brown sugar mixed with 2 tablespoons of dry mustard. Decorate with pineapple slices and whole cloves. Brown at 375 degrees for 15 minutes. Allow to cool before slicing. Wrap the ham tightly in aluminum foil and refrigerate. Do not use plastic wrap as it holds too much moisture and speeds spoilage. Cooked country ham will keep in the refrigerator up to six weeks.

Chocolate Chip Cake

18 1/4-ounce box yellow cake mix
3-ounce package instant vanilla pudding
3-ounce package instant chocolate pudding
4 eggs
1 1/2 cups water
1/2 cup oil
6-ounce package chocolate chips

Combine the cake mix and puddings in a large bowl; stir until mixed. Add the eggs, water and oil; blend well. Beat for 2 minutes at medium speed. Add the chocolate chips and stir using a spoon. Pour into a coated and floured bundt pan. Bake at 325 degrees for 1 hour. Ice with your favorite frosting or sprinkle with powdered sugar.

MENU

Odds on the Meal

Party Beef Balls...94

Chicken and Wild Rice Soup...95

Victory Spinach Salad...97

Chicken with
    Spinach and Mushrooms...98

Brown Rice with Shredded Carrots...100

Chocolate Delight...101

Beef Balls

1 1/2 to 2 pounds ground beef
1 tablespoon Worcestershire sauce
1/4 teaspoon garlic powder
1/4 pound grated Cheddar cheese
1 egg
1/2 cup ketchup
1/2 teaspoon horseradish

Combine all of the ingredients and roll into bite-size balls. Place the balls on an uncoated cookie sheet. Bake at 350 degrees for 20 minutes.

Chicken and Wild Rice Soup

1 cup uncooked quick-cooking wild rice
1 cup chopped onion
2 cloves garlic, minced
3 cups chicken broth
1 1/2 cups peeled, cubed baking potato
3 cups milk
1/3 cup all-purpose flour
10 ounces processed cheese, cubed
2 cups cooked, chopped chicken breasts
1/2 teaspoon freshly ground black pepper
1/4 teaspoon salt
1/4 cup chopped fresh parsley

Cook the rice according to the package directions, omitting the salt and butter. Coat a large Dutch oven and heat over a medium-high heat. Add the onion and garlic; sauté for 3 minutes. Add the broth and potato; bring to a boil over a medium-high heat. Cover, reduce the heat, and simmer for 5 minutes or until the potato is tender. Combine the milk and flour, stirring well using a whisk. Add the milk mixture to the potato mixture; cook for 5 minutes or until slightly thick, stirring constantly. Remove from the heat; add the cheese, stirring until the cheese melts. Stir in the rice, chicken, pepper, and salt. Garnish with parsley, if desired.

Makes 8 servings.

Victory *Spinach Salad*

**Two 10-ounce packages fresh spinach,
    washed, drained and torn into
    bite-size pieces**
Two 12-ounce cartons cottage cheese
1 cup chopped pecans
1 cup sour cream
1/2 cup sugar
4 tablespoons vinegar
4 tablespoons horseradish
1 teaspoon dry mustard
1/2 teaspoon salt

Layer the spinach, cottage cheese and pecans in
a large serving bowl. Combine the sour cream,
sugar, vinegar, horseradish, mustard and salt in
a separate bowl; pour over the spinach mixture.

Serves 8.

97

Chicken

with Spinach and Mushrooms

5-ounce package fresh baby spinach
3 boneless, skinless chicken breasts
Salt and pepper to taste
Onion powder to taste
Garlic powder to taste
8 large mushrooms, chopped
7 cherry tomatoes, halved
4 tablespoons butter
1 cup grated Parmesan cheese
1 cup heavy cream
1/4 teaspoon curry powder

Place the spinach in a coated 9x13-inch baking dish. Slice the chicken in 2-inch strips and sprinkle with the salt, pepper, onion powder and garlic powder. Place the chicken over the top of the spinach. Place the mushrooms and tomatoes over the top of the chicken. Melt the butter in a large skillet and add the cheese. Cook over a medium heat until the cheese melts. Add the cream and cook about 5 minutes, stirring until all is well blended. Add the curry, stir and pour over the mixture over the chicken. Bake at 350 degrees for 45 to 60 minutes. Serve over Brown Rice with Shredded Carrots.

Serves 4.

Brown Rice with Shredded Carrots

2 cups instant brown rice
2 cups water
2 teaspoons beef bouillon
1 cup shredded carrots

Combine the rice, water, beef bouillon and carrots in a saucepan. Cook over a high heat until the mixture boils. Reduce the heat to low and continue to cook, covered, for about 15 minutes or until all the liquid is absorbed.

Serves 4.

Chocolate Delight

1 cup all-purpose flour
1 stick margarine
1 cup finely chopped pecans
8-ounce package cream cheese, softened
1 cup powdered sugar
1 cup whipped topping
Two 3-ounce packages instant chocolate pudding
2 cups cold milk
Whipped topping
Chopped pecans

Combine the flour, margarine and pecans in a bowl; mix using a fork. Press the mixture into the bottom of a 9x13-inch baking dish. Bake at 300 degrees for 25 minutes or until lightly browned. Set aside to cool. Combine the cream cheese and powdered sugar; mix well. Add the 1 cup whipped topping. Spread the mixture over the cooled crust. Blend the chocolate pudding and milk using a mixer on low speed. Spread on top of the cream cheese mixture. Spread a thin layer of the whipped topping over the top and sprinkle with the chopped pecans.

Off Track Temptations

Mint Julep Punch...104

BLT Dip...107

Celebration Cheese Wafers...108

Mint Julep Punch

12-ounce jar mint jelly
2 cups water
46-ounce can unsweetened pineapple juice
1/2 cup lime juice
2 cups water
28-ounce bottle lemon-lime soda
1 liter Kentucky bourbon
Lime slices
Fresh mint leaves

Combine the jelly and 2 cups of the water in a saucepan over a low heat and stir until the jelly melts; let cool. Add the pineapple juice, lime juice and the remaining 2 cups water. Pour into a container and chill. Pour the juice mixture and bourbon over ice in a punch bowl. Pour the lemon-lime soda in slowly and gently stir. Garnish with the lime slices and fresh mint leaves, if desired.

Makes 5 quarts or 32 servings.

This punch may be made without the bourbon, if desired.

BLT Dip

1 cup sour cream
1 cup mayonnaise
1 cup shredded Cheddar cheese
1 cup seeded, chopped tomatoes
3-ounce package bacon bits
1 tablespoon chopped green onion

Combine the sour cream, mayonnaise, cheese, tomatoes and bacon in a bowl; chill until ready to serve. Garnish with the green onion. Serve with crackers or vegetables.

Celebration Cheese Wafers

1/2 pound grated extra-sharp Cheddar cheese
1 stick butter, softened
1/8 teaspoon cayenne pepper
1 1/2 cups self-rising flour, divided
Whole or pecan halves
Paprika

Combine the cheese and butter in the food processor and mix well. Add the pepper and 3/4 cup of the flour and mix again. Add the remaining flour and process until the mixture becomes a ball. Pinch off small amounts of the dough and roll into balls. Press the balls down on an uncoated baking sheet and top with a pecan. Dust lightly with the paprika and bake at 350 degrees for about 12 minutes. Remove from the oven and cool. Store in an airtight container.

Makes about 4 dozen wafers.

MENU

Place Bet
or
Show Samples

Apple Dandy
  Breakfast Sandwiches...110

Fresh Tomato Pie...111

Swiss Cheese Grits...112

Long Shot Scalloped Apples...115

Apple Dandy Breakfast Sandwiches

White bread slices, toasted
Margarine
Processed cheese slices
Thin apple slices
Brown sugar
Crisp-fried bacon slices

Spread each toast slice with the margarine. Cover each with a cheese slice and apple slices. Sprinkle each with the brown sugar and broil until the cheese is melted. Top with the bacon and serve.

Fresh Tomato Pie

One 9-inch pie crust
5 to 6 ripe tomatoes or 8 to 10 Roma tomatoes, thickly sliced
1/2-ounce package fresh basil, cut with scissors
4 to 5 tablespoons chopped fresh chives
1/4 cup mayonnaise
1 1/2 cups shredded Cheddar cheese

Place the pie crust in a deep-dish pie plate and
partially bake according to the package directions.
Divide the tomato slices, basil and chives and
layer each item until the crust is filled.
Combine the mayonnaise and cheese in
a bowl. Spread the mixture over the top.
Sprinkle with additional Cheddar cheese.
Bake at 400 degrees for 35 minutes.

Serves 6 to 8.

Swiss Cheese Grits

1 quart milk
1 cup quick grits
1/2 pound butter
1 cup grated Swiss cheese
1 teaspoon salt
1/2 teaspoon pepper
1 cup crushed cornflakes
1/3 cup grated Parmesan cheese

Bring the milk to a boil in a saucepan. Add the grits, slowly, and stir for about 3 minutes or until thick. Remove from the heat; add the butter, Swiss cheese, salt and pepper. Spoon the mixture into a buttered 9x10-inch baking dish. Top with the cornflakes and Parmesan cheese. Bake at 350 degrees for 30 minutes.

Makes 8 servings.

Scalloped Apples

2 cups bread crumbs
1/4 cup melted butter
1/4 cup brown sugar
Dash of salt
1/4 teaspoon nutmeg
1/4 teaspoon allspice
4 cups cooking apples, peeled,
    cored and diced
2 tablespoons lemon juice
1/2 cup hot apple juice

Combine the bread crumbs, butter, brown sugar, salt, nutmeg and allspice. Place half of the crumb mixture into a shallow buttered baking dish. Add the apples, then the remaining crumbs. Mix the lemon juice and apple juice and pour over all. Bake at 350 degrees for 30 minutes or until the crumbs are brown and the apples are tender. Time will depend on firmness of the apples.

Makes 6 servings.

MENU High Stakes Sensations

Triple Crown Taco Soup...119

Marinated Cauliflower Salad...120

Baked Salmon...123

Asparagus with
   Caramelized Onions and Bacon...125

Run for the Roses Pie...126

Triple Crown
Taco Soup

1 pound ground chuck
1 large onion, chopped
Two 151/2-ounce cans kidney beans, undrained
15 1/2-ounce can pinto beans, undrained
15 1/2-ounce can whole kernel corn, undrained
15 1/2-ounce can tomato sauce
15 1/2-ounce can diced tomatoes, undrained
4.5-ounce can chopped green chiles
1/4-ounce envelope taco seasoning mix
1-ounce envelope ranch dressing mix
1/2 teaspoon cumin
1/2 teaspoon minced garlic
15 1/2-ounce can beef broth
1 beef broth can of water
Salt and pepper to taste

Toppings:

Corn chips
Shredded lettuce
Chopped tomato
Sour cream
Shredded Cheddar cheese

Cook the beef and onion in a Dutch oven until the meat is brown and onion is tender, stir until the meat crumbles; drain. Add the beans, corn, tomato sauce, tomatoes, green chiles, taco seasoning, ranch dressing, cumin, garlic, beef broth, water, salt and pepper; bring to a boil. Reduce the heat and simmer, uncovered, for 15 minutes stirring occasionally. Spoon the soup into bowls and top with desired toppings.

Marinated Cauliflower Salad

1 head cauliflower, broken into florets
1 large green pepper, seeded and cut into thin strips
1 large red onion, peeled and sliced into rings
1 pint cherry tomatoes
1 package Good Seasons cheese garlic dressing

Steam the cauliflower until tender-crisp. Place the cauliflower in a large salad bowl and add the green pepper strips, onion rings and cherry tomatoes. Prepare the seasoning mix according to the package directions. Pour the dressing over the vegetables; cover and marinate overnight. Stir to coat vegetables before serving.

Baked Salmon

1 small onion, finely chopped
2 cloves garlic, minced
2 tablespoons olive oil, divided
2 chopped tomatoes
2 small zucchini, cut into 1/4-inch pieces
2 teaspoons oregano
Salt and pepper to taste
Four 5-ounce salmon fillets
2 ounces grated Parmesan cheese
2 ounces grated Cheddar cheese

Sauté the onion and garlic with 1 tablespoon of the olive oil for 5 minutes. Add the tomatoes, zucchini, oregano, salt and pepper and the remaining olive oil. Cook for 8 to 10 minutes. Place the fish in a buttered baking dish. Top with the vegetable mixture. Combine the two cheeses and spread over the top. Bake at 350 degrees for 20 to 25 minutes.

Serves 4.

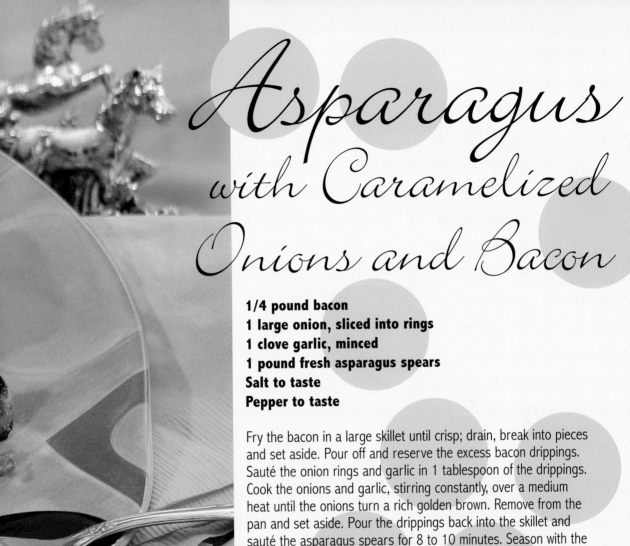

Asparagus
with Caramelized
Onions and Bacon

1/4 pound bacon
1 large onion, sliced into rings
1 clove garlic, minced
1 pound fresh asparagus spears
Salt to taste
Pepper to taste

Fry the bacon in a large skillet until crisp; drain, break into pieces and set aside. Pour off and reserve the excess bacon drippings. Sauté the onion rings and garlic in 1 tablespoon of the drippings. Cook the onions and garlic, stirring constantly, over a medium heat until the onions turn a rich golden brown. Remove from the pan and set aside. Pour the drippings back into the skillet and sauté the asparagus spears for 8 to 10 minutes. Season with the salt and pepper. The asparagus should remain crunchy but still be cooked through. Remove from the heat. Place in a serving bowl, top with the onions and sprinkle with the bacon.

Serves 4.

125

Run For The Roses

Pie

1 cup sugar
1/2 cup all-purpose flour
1/2 cup melted butter
2 slightly beaten eggs
3/4 cup chopped pecans
6 ounces semisweet chocolate chips
1 teaspoon vanilla extract
2 tablespoons Kentucky bourbon
9-inch unbaked pie crust

Combine the sugar and flour in a large bowl;
mix in the butter. Add the eggs, pecans,
chocolate chips, vanilla extract and bourbon;
mix well. Pour into the pie crust. Place the
pie on a baking sheet and bake at 325
degrees for 55 minutes or until the top is
golden brown.

Serves 8.

Photo Finish Buffet

Black-eyed Pea Soup...131

Creole Squash...133

Bourbon Pork Chops...134

Summertime Peach Pie...135

Black-eyed Pea Soup

Two 15 1/2-ounce cans black-eyed peas, undrained
15 1/2-ounce can of water
10-ounce can Rotel diced tomatoes
1 cup cooked rice
1 teaspoon seasoned salt
Salt and pepper to taste
1 pound sausage
1 large onion, chopped
1 large bell pepper, chopped

Combine the black-eyed peas, water, tomatoes, rice, seasoned salt, salt and pepper in a large pan. Brown the sausage, onion and bell pepper in a skillet; drain and add to the black-eyed pea mixture. Simmer for 30 minutes. Serve topped with salsa.

Creole Squash

**2 pounds yellow or zucchini squash,
thinly sliced**
2 onions, thinly sliced
2 cups canned diced tomatoes
1 tablespoon prepared mustard
1/2 teaspoon salt
Pepper to taste
1 cup grated Cheddar cheese

Arrange the squash slices in a lightly coated
baking dish. Layer the onion slices on top of the
squash. Combine the tomatoes, mustard, salt
and pepper; pour over the squash and onions.
Bake at 350 degrees for 45 minutes. Cover with
the grated cheese and return to the oven until
the cheese melts.

Bourbon Pork Chops

3 packed tablespoons brown sugar
3 tablespoons soy sauce
3 tablespoons Kentucky bourbon
1/4 teaspoon ground ginger
Four 3/4-inch pork chops

Combine the sugar, soy sauce, bourbon and ginger in a shallow baking dish; mix well. Add the pork chops and marinate for at least 4 hours. Grill and baste, turning often.

Summertime Peach Pie

3 to 4 large fresh peaches, peeled and sliced
1/4 cup brown sugar
1 1/2 cups crushed gingersnap cookies
4 tablespoons butter, melted
1 cup sugar
8 ounces cream cheese, at room temperature
8 ounces whipped topping, at room temperature

Place the sliced peaches in a bowl, sprinkle with the brown sugar and turn to coat. Allow the peaches to sit. Combine the crushed cookies and butter; mix well. Pat the mixture into the bottom of a 9-inch pie dish. Bake at 350 degrees for about 12 minutes. Remove from the oven and cool. Combine the sugar and cream cheese in a food processor and mix well. Add the whipped topping and pulse until mixed. Pour the peaches into the crust and cover with the cream cheese mixture. Spread evenly, cover and refrigerate overnight.

Serves 8.

Index

Appetizers

Benedictine, 10
BLT Dip, 107
Celebration Cheese Wafers, 108
Country Ham Balls, 20
Jockey Spicy Snack Mix, 29
Kentucky Krispies, 66
Party Beef Balls, 94
Smoked Salmon, 10
Spicy Brie, 87

Beverages

Bloody Mary Pitcher, 65
Mint Julep Punch, 104
Race Day Sippers, 37
Silky Sunshine, 29
Spring Morning Mimosas, 44
Traditional Mint Julep, 9

Breads, Breakfast and Brunch

Apple Dandy Breakfast Sandwiches, 110
Bourbon Bread, 11
Break Away Breakfast Sandwich, 78
Breakfast Fruit Salad, 38
Derby Day Biscuits, 78
Fast Break French Toast Bake, 39
In the Lead Sausage and Grits, 22
Out of the Gate Ham Biscuits, 45
Skillet Coffee Cake, 80
Sun Shines Bright Strawberry Bread, 20
Winning Ticket Breakfast Casserole, 46

Desserts

After the Race Apple Squares, 24
Bourbon Brownies, 34
Bourbon Cake, 69
Chocolate Chip Cake, 90
Chocolate Delight, 101
Chocolate Kentucky Bourbon Balls, 12
Infield Cherry Freeze, 40
Kentucky Sheet Cake, 18
Long Shot Scalloped Apples, 115
Mint Julep Cheesecake, 55
Peppermint Dessert, 61
Post Race Hot Brownie, 75
Run for the Roses Pie, 126
Summertime Peach Pie, 135
Thoroughbred Peach Cobbler, 48

Entrées

Baked Salmon, 123
Beef Parmesan, 53
Bourbon Pork Chops, 134
Chicken with Spinach and Mushrooms, 98
Down the Stretch Bourbon Salmon, 32
Hall of Fame Pork Chops, 16
Horse Racing Hot Brown, 67
Shrimp Milano, 72
Traditional Kentucky County Ham, 89
Winner's Circle Shrimp and Artichoke Pasta, 60

Salads

Bleu Cheese Cole Slaw, 59
Down to the Wire Pasta Salad, 31
Fast Break Black Bean and Rice Salad, 15
Marinated Cauliflower Salad, 120
Quarter Mile Cole Slaw, 51
Victory Spinach Salad, 97

Side Items

Asparagus with Caramelized Onions
   and Bacon, 125
Brown Rice with Shredded Carrots, 100
Creole Squash, 133
Derby Day Cheese Soufflé, 23
Fresh Tomato Pie, 111
Lucky Day Green Beans, 32
Marinated Asparagus, 68
Mushrooms Florentine, 73
Swiss Cheese Grits, 112

Soups

Around the Turn Beer Cheese Soup, 14
Baked Potato Soup, 88
Black-eyed Pea Soup, 131
Bluegrass Mushroom Soup, 50
Chicken and Wild Rice Soup, 95
Cream of Asparagus Soup, 58
Hot Brown Soup, 30
Triple Crown Taco Soup, 119